Daily Reflections from

Dr David R. Hawkins

Also by
Dr David R. Hawkins

*Book of Slides: The Complete Collection Presented
at the 2002–2011 Lectures with Clarifications*

*The Map of Consciousness Explained:
A Proven Energy Scale to Actualize Your Ultimate Potential*

*The Ego Is Not the Real You: Wisdom to
Transcend the Mind and Realize the Self*

Audio Program

The Map of Consciousness Explained

How to Surrender to God

Live Life as a Prayer

Please visit:

Hay House UK: www.hayhouse.co.uk
Hay House USA: www.hayhouse.com®
Hay House Australia: www.hayhouse.com.au
Hay House India: www.hayhouse.co.in

Daily Reflections from

Dr David R. Hawkins

365
CONTEMPLATIONS
on Surrender, Healing
and Consciousness

HAY HOUSE

Carlsbad, California • New York City
London • Sydney • New Delhi

Published in the United Kingdom by:
Hay House UK Ltd, The Sixth Floor, Watson House,
54 Baker Street, London W1U 7BU
Tel: +44 (0)20 3927 7290; Fax: +44 (0)20 3927 7291; www.hayhouse.co.uk

Published in the United States of America by:
Hay House Inc., PO Box 5100, Carlsbad, CA 92018-5100 Tel: (1) 760 431 7695
or (800) 654 5126
Fax: (1) 760 431 6948 or (800) 650 5115; www.hayhouse.com

Published in Australia by:
Hay House Australia Ltd, 18/36 Ralph St, Alexandria NSW 2015 Tel: (61) 2
9669 4299; Fax: (61) 2 9669 4144; www.hayhouse.com.au

Published in India by:
Hay House Publishers India, Muskaan Complex, Plot No.3, B-2, Vasant Kunj,
New Delhi 110 070
Tel: (91) 11 4176 1620; Fax: (91) 11 4176 1630; www.hayhouse.co.in

A catalogue record for this book is available from the British Library.

Tradepaper ISBN: 978-1-78817-685-9
E-Book ISBN: 978-1-4019-6510-5

Gloria in Excelsis Deo!

Preface

Each step along the way to enlightenment is exciting and rewarding when its essence is revealed. Taken out of context, any critical insight can seem baffling, yet intriguing. For each seeker, there are important key understandings that light the way and facilitate success. This is a collection of such truths that serve as fulcrums for major leaps forward. Although there are many doorways to heaven, each seeker must find his or her own route.

Comprehension at great depths unravels the essential truth of seeming complexity. It is said that there are 10,000 ways to God, yet they can all be reduced to certain critical elements common to all successful pathways. Therefore, each of the accompanying quotes is proven to be of great value.

— Bon voyage!
David R. Hawkins, M.D., Ph.D.

Introduction

The destiny of the spirit will be, for better or worse, depending on the choices and decisions one makes.

That quote is one of the "daily reflections" in this book. Dr. Hawkins is reminding us that whatever we choose in our daily life directly impacts the destiny of our spirit. What will you choose to do today? What thoughts will you allow to circulate in your headspace today? Where will you choose to focus your attention? Those choices of inner and outer life, day by day, determine the destiny of your spirit.

Thus, we see the great value of a book like this, because it gives us a daily orientation. For each day, we have a passage to contemplate. If we make time for this daily reflection, and if we allow it to sink deeply into our spirit, then our day is pointed in a positive direction. We may fall on our face; no one is perfect. But a daily spiritual reflection helps us in that moment to get up and not give up.

Dr. Hawkins told me one time, when I asked him about the significance of his life's work, that it's like an enzyme:

"This information on consciousness has the power to diagnose and resolve all spiritual blocks and ailments. It functions like an 'enzyme' of spiritual facilitation. Upon contact, this 'enzyme' potentiates the inborn mechanisms of self-awareness and self-healing." This little book of daily reflections, then, provides the spiritual 'enzyme' that will help you digest the phenomena of your day into something that benefits your spirit.

This comment from Dr. Hawkins reminds me of meeting with the Missionaries of Charity nuns at Mother Teresa's convent in Rome. They invited us there for Mother Teresa's canonization to sainthood, in 2016, at the Vatican. We toured the "Home for the Poor," where they lived out their vow to give "wholehearted service to the poorest of the poor." Day in and day out, the nuns live among the sick and dying, the rejected ones that no one else will care for. The place was full of love. We asked the sisters, "How do you do this every day? Where do you get your energy?" They told us that, every day, they have four hours of prayer, including meditation on the Word of God, Holy Mass where they receive the Eucharist, and a Holy Hour where they adore Jesus in the Blessed Sacrament. Their lives are woven with the Presence of Christ in the Eucharist, and this is the fuel for their work. They said: "Without the daily hours of prayer and the Eucharist, it is just ourselves we give to the poor, not God."

We see that every spiritual pathway has a daily practice to keep the seeker aligned with their spirit's destiny. Early on in the path, we may strive for the goals of self-improvement or reaching a high spiritual state. Then, as we go along the path, we lay down "the goal-seeking of the spiritual ego" (Dr. Hawkins's words). While he walked among us, Dr. Hawkins gave us a premier example of the depth of self-surrender that is the hallmark of the true sage. In this little book, he leaves his footprints for us to follow: "*To be the servant of God becomes one's goal rather than enlightenment. To be a perfect channel for God's love is to surrender completely . . .*"

We pray that this book will help you, every day, to choose peace and love over all other options. "Straight and narrow is the path, waste no time."

—Fran Grace, Ph.D.

January 1

It is of little benefit to be personally self-critical or think that one "should" be farther along the road than one is. Spiritual evolution is irregular, and at times often seems sporadic and at other times stationary. Realize that guilt is a narcissistic indulgence.

January 2

Whatever we do from the space of inner knowing is certain before it even happens. When we're on the right track, we have that absolute inner certainty of knowing, and the outcome is already obvious to us.

January 3

It is well to keep in mind at all times that the ego/mind does not experience the world but only its own perception of it.

January 4

Existence is its own reward. It is more gratifying in the long term to fulfill potentiality than to try to achieve results. Therefore, one becomes aligned with excellence of performance for its own sake.

January 5

It is set in legend that the Buddha passed on enlightenment without saying a word to his follower Mahakasyapa. At that great moment in history, Buddha silently handed him a flower, and in that moment, Mahakasyapa became enlightened. There was no striving, trying, practicing, or straining for enlightenment. There was none of that left-brain stuff. It was a sudden "aha," completely and totally an "experience."

January 6

All "problems" are products of mental processing only and do not exist in the world.

January 7

To win in life means to give up the obsession of "who's at fault." Graciousness is far more powerful than belligerence. It is better to succeed than to win.

January 8

Human progress is evolutionary, and, therefore, mistakes and errors are inevitable. The only real tragedy is to become older but not wiser.

January 9

To consistently choose love, peace, or forgiveness leads one out of the house of mirrors.

January 10

Through compassion arises the desire to understand rather than condemn.

January 11

Forgiveness is an extremely important major tool, especially when it is combined with the willingness of humility and acceptance of human fallibility and susceptibility to error. From spiritual intention, the surrendering of egoistic options may seem like a sacrifice—but when recontextualized, they are revealed to be a hidden gift.

January 12

The best attitude is one of devotion to truth rather than being contentious toward falsehood. Open-minded curiosity leads to progressive discovery of information never before available, which may therefore seem confrontational upon first exposure.

January 13

We can't own that which is great within ourselves unless we learn to recognize it in others.

January 14

If the essential dynamic of one's spiritual seeking is not spiritual ambition (to get somewhere) but the progressive surrender of the obstacles to love, then that which is called "spiritual ego" doesn't arise as an obstacle later.

January 15

Every advance that we make in our awareness benefits unseen multitudes and strengthens the next step for others to follow. Every act of kindness is noticed by the universe and is preserved forever.

January 16

The common element of most fears is that they are based on the illusion that happiness is dependent on externals and therefore vulnerable. To overcome the illusion of vulnerability brings great relief and the correction of being run by fear. Life becomes benign and filled with satisfaction and an easygoing, confident attitude, instead of constant guardedness.

January 17

At every instant, one is really making a choice between heaven or hell. The cumulative effect of all these choices determines the calibrated level of consciousness and one's karmic and spiritual fate.

January 18

The processing out of anger requires inner honesty and the willingness to surrender what is lacking integrity and essentially unworkable, and replace it with self-confidence. Compensatory attitudes that are far more powerful than anger are dedication, reason, humility, gratitude, perseverance, and tolerance.

January 19

By its nature, the pathway to God is not easy. It requires considerable courage, fortitude, willingness, and forbearance. It is strengthened by humility and a benign conscience.

January 20

In true success there is no time delay. The reward is instantaneous, so that the entire process is a rewarding one. Success is feeling good about what we do.

January 21

The development of a spiritual ego can be avoided by the realization that spiritual progress is the result of God's grace, not the result of one's personal endeavors.

January 22

Persistent devotion to spiritual truth and love allows for the dissolution of resistances.

January 23

Reality needs no agreement. Reality is not an acquisition, but is instead a purely spontaneous, subjective realization when the positionalities of the dualistic ego are surrendered.

January 24

The evolution is to turn one's life into a prayer/contemplation/meditation/supplication and surrender. One's life becomes the prayer—the prayer is the contemplation.

January 25

This moment is the only reality that is being experienced; all else is an abstraction and a mental construct. Therefore, one cannot actually live 70 years at all; only this exact, fleeting moment is possible.

January 26

The mature mind knows that it is evolving and that growth and development are satisfying and pleasurable in and of themselves. Maturity implies that one has learned how to be comfortable with uncertainty and has included it as a legitimate ingredient. Uncertainty leads to discovery, whereas skepticism is stultifying.

January 27

It is of great value to select a basic dictum to live by, such as the decision to be kind and of goodwill toward all life in all its expressions.

January 28

Once the worst of all possible fears—the dread and shock of death—has been faced, it is superseded by a profound sense of serenity, peace, oneness, and immunity from fear.

January 29

Commitment is to the core of truth itself and is free of seduction by proselytization or secrecies. All that is necessary is curiosity and an attraction to truth, which is complete, total, and self-sufficient.

January 30

Subjectively, all that is needed to progress are patience, prayer, faith in the process, and the surrendering of resistance. Confusion, like a change in the weather, is a transitional condition that clears with patience and also with emergence into the next stage, whereby the confusing condition is transcended.

January 31

Actions are the automatic consequence of the integration of context, field, and intention. All action is actually spontaneous and reflects karmic propensities and local conditions that may or may not favor expression. To depersonalize actions, it is only necessary to let go of the belief that there is a separate, independent causal agent called "I" or "me."

February 1

True generosity expects no reward, for there are no strings attached.

February 2

Begin by accepting the very important statement that all truth is subjective. Do not waste lifetimes looking for an objective truth because no such thing exists. Even if it did, it could not be found except by the purely subjective experience of it. All knowledge and wisdom are subjective. Nothing can be said to exist unless it is subjectively experienced.

February 3

Accept that all sentient beings live by faith. Despite naïve and pretentious claims to the contrary, all people live solely by the principle of faith—it is only a question of faith in *what*. Faith can be placed in the illusory, the intellect, reason, science, progress, political and worldly power, ego satisfactions, pleasure, wealth, or hope (such as "tomorrow").

February 4

To surrender what one thinks one is to God does not leave one as "nothing," but quite the contrary: it leads to the discovery that one is everything.

February 5

Spiritual development is not an accomplishment but a way of life. It is an orientation that brings its own rewards, and what is important is the direction of one's motives.

February 6

The willingness to look at a fear and work with it until we are free of it brings about immediate rewards.

February 7

With spiritual maturity, one understands that this lifetime is precious and too valuable to waste on the ideas of being superior or other ego-inflating, vainglorious illusions.

February 8

To contribute to the welfare and happiness of others is gratifying and leads to the discovery that generosity is its own reward.

February 9

Objectively, it can be seen that thoughts really belong to the consciousness of the world; the individual mind merely processes them in new combinations and permutations. What seem to be truly original thoughts appear only through the medium of genius and are invariably felt by their authors to be a gift, found or given, not self-created. It may be the case that we're each unique, as no two snowflakes are alike . . . however, *we're still just snowflakes.*

February 10

Like any limiting ego position, it is not the position itself that requires relinquishment but the emotional payoff or energy that holding on to that position provides to the ego.

February 11

To sincerely dedicate oneself to be a servant of the Lord and ask what is His will is sufficient. The answers reveal themselves without necessarily even having to be formulated. To be "spiritual" simply means an intention.

February 12

Peace is absolutely a choice and a decision, although not a popular one in our society, despite all the rhetoric about the term. The decision to overlook the seeming inequities of life instead of reacting to them is certainly a choice.

February 13

As we get closer to the discovery of the source of the ego's tenacity, we make the amazing critical discovery that *we are enamored with ourselves.*

February 14

The world can only see us as we see ourselves . . .
Picture yourself as being generous, forgiving, loving, and experiencing your inner greatness. Instantly, there will be an enormous increase in muscle strength indicating a surge of positive bio-energy.

February 15

Great leaps in levels of consciousness are always preceded by surrender of the illusion that "I know."

February 16

Every act of kindness, consideration, forgiveness, or love affects everyone.

February 17

All spiritual truth is contained in every spiritual concept. It is only necessary to completely and totally understand *one single concept* to understand all of them in order to arrive at the realization of the Real.

February 18

The higher the level of consciousness, the greater the likelihood that what is held in mind will actualize. Thus, to see solutions that "serve the highest goal" is more powerful than simply projecting fulfillment of merely personal selfish desires and gain.

February 19

Serious inner spiritual work may sound tedious and demanding (to the ego), but is exciting to the spirit, which is eager to return home. Consciousness innately seeks its source.

February 20

Until one acknowledges the intrinsic genius within oneself, one will have great difficulty recognizing it in others— we can only acknowledge *without* what we realize *within*.

February 21

The impossible becomes possible as soon as we are totally surrendered. This is because wanting blocks receiving it and results in a fear of not getting it. The energy of desire is, in essence, a denial that what we want is ours for the asking.

February 22

The level of consciousness is determined by the choices made by the spiritual will, and therefore is the consequence as well as the determinant of karma. Freedom to evolve requires a world that affords the greatest opportunity to ascend or descend the spiritual ladder. Viewed from that perspective, this is an ideal world, and its society is constituted by a wide range of experiential options.

February 23

In a higher state of consciousness, our experience of the universe changes. It now becomes like a giving, loving, unconditionally approving parent who wants us to have everything we want, and it is ours for the asking. This is creating a different context. It is giving the universe a different meaning.

February 24

Frustration results from exaggerating the importance of desires.

February 25

Out of an unrestricted love for God arises the willingness to surrender all motives except to serve God completely. To be the servant of God becomes one's goal rather than enlightenment. To be a perfect channel for God's love is to surrender completely and to eliminate the goal seeking of the spiritual ego. Joy itself becomes the initiator of further spiritual work.

February 26

Everything we do and say, every movement we make, is energized by the lovingness that we have owned within ourselves. Whether speaking to a large audience or petting the dog, the energy of love is felt to be pouring out. We want to share what we hold in the heart as an experiential knowingness, and we hold it in the heart for everyone and everything, that they would be feeling it, too. We pray for that inner experience of infinite love for everyone around us, including the animals. Our life is a blessing to everything around us. We acknowledge to others and to our animals the gift that they are to us.

February 27

Emotion is not an indicator of truth, as it is both reflective and determinative of positionalities and conditioning.

February 28

Truth is recognized. It presents itself to a field of aware-ness that has been prepared in order to allow the pre-sentation to reveal itself. Truth and enlightenment are not acquired or achieved. They are states or conditions that present themselves when the conditions are appropriate.

February 29

A useful approach is to let the love for God replace the willfulness that is driving the seeking. One can release all desire to seek and realize that the thought that there is anything else but God is a baseless vanity. This is the same vanity that claims authorship for one's experiences, thoughts, and actions. With reflection, it can be seen that both the body and the mind are the result of the innumer-able conditions of the universe, and that one is at best the witness of this concordance.

March 1

When the clouds are removed, the sun shines forth and we discover that peace was the truth all along.

March 2

The linear domain entails suffering; thus, the best Teachers throughout history taught the ways of salvation or enlightenment as the only answer to escape from that suffering.

March 3

It takes inner discipline and surrender of attitudes not to fall into the temptation of identifying with a position about world events.

March 4

Even the decision to turn one's life over to God brings joy and gives life a whole new meaning. It becomes uplifting, and the greater context gives life more significance and reward. One eventually becomes unwilling to support negativity, within or without. This is not because it is wrong, but merely futile. Although the journey to God begins with failure and doubt, it progresses into certainty. The way is really quite simple.

March 5

By inner humility plus wisdom, the seeker of truth takes serious note of the inherent limitations of the human psyche itself and no longer relies on the impressionable personal ego as its sole arbiter of truth.

March 6

Everything in the universe constantly gives off an iden-
tifiable energy pattern of a specific frequency that remains
for all time and can be read by those who know how. Every
word, deed, and intention creates a permanent record;
every thought is known and recorded forever. There
are no secrets; nothing is hidden, nor can it be. Everyone lives in the public domain. Our spirits stand naked in
time for all to see. Everyone's life, finally, is accountable to
the universe.

March 7

If we examine much of what the world traditionally calls "evil," what we discover is not evil, which is an
abstraction, epithet, and label. Instead, we see behaviors
that could be described as primitive, infantile, egotistical,
narcissistic, selfish, and ignorant, complicated by the psy-
chological mechanisms of denial, projection, and paranoia
in order to justify hatred.

March 8

All that we experience are our own thoughts, feelings, and beliefs projected onto the world, actually causing what we see to happen.

Most people have experienced all the different levels of consciousness at one time or another but, in general, we tend to operate primarily at one level or another for long periods of time. Most people are preoccupied with survival in all its subtle forms, and so they reflect primarily fear, anger, and a desire for gain. They have not learned that the state of lovingness is the most powerful of all survival tools.

March 9

The only way to enhance one's power in the world is by increasing one's integrity, understanding, and capacity for compassion.

March 10

When one realizes that one is the universe, complete and at one with All That Is, forever without end, no further suffering is possible.

March 11

The greater the challenge, the greater the development of inner strength, decision, and determination. By persistence and discipline, it can be seen that temptation is an option to merely refuse rather than an impulse that calls for attack or negation.

March 12

Appreciate that every step forward benefits everyone. One's spiritual dedication and work is a gift to life and the love of mankind.

March 13

The mature spiritual aspirant is one who has explored the ego's options and false promises of happiness.

March 14

Without a change of consciousness, there is no real reduction of stress. Only the consequences are ameliorated. All of these after-the-fact techniques and treatments do help and often alleviate a given condition and bring some relief, but they leave the basis of the problem untouched. One can follow all of these techniques and yet remain the same stress-prone person. In our experience, the conscious use of the mechanism of surrender is more effective in addressing chronic stress-related illnesses. Illnesses begin to heal spontaneously because the underlying emotional cause has been removed, and further treatments often become unnecessary.

March 15

To even hear of enlightenment is already the rarest of gifts. Anyone who has ever heard of enlightenment will never be satisfied with anything else.

March 16

Along the spiritual pathway, blocks and temptations appear, as do doubts and fears. Classically, they have been termed the "tests" that arise from the ego, which does not relish relinquishment of dominion. These are overcome by reaffirmation of goals and commitment, as well as by reinforcing counterbalancing principles such as dedication, tenacity, constancy, courage, conviction, and intention.

March 17

Peace comes with total inner surrender to *what is*.

March 18

Enlightenment is not a condition to be obtained; it is merely a certainty to be surrendered to, for the Self is already one's Reality. It is the Self that is attracting one to spiritual information.

March 19

The ego/mind presumes and is convinced that its perceptions and interpretations of life experiences are the "real" thing and therefore "true." It also believes by projection that other people see, think, and feel the same way; and if they do not, they are mistaken and therefore wrong. Thus, perception reinforces its hold by reification and presumptions.

March 20

To strive to know God is in itself pristine and the ultimate aspiration.

March 21

The decisions to "be kind to all of life" or to respect the sacredness of all that exists are powerful attitudes in spiritual evolution, along with the virtues of compassion, the willingness to forgive, and seeking to understand rather than to judge. By constantly surrendering, perceptions dissolve into the discernment of essence.

March 22

By virtue of devotion, there is alignment with inner integrity that results in the self-honesty and conviction necessary to transcend the seduction of transitory emotional payoffs of the intransigent ego.

March 23

Like springtime, the promise of a new era in man's understanding of God is emerging. Now the level of consciousness of mankind is high enough to be able to recognize the truth of a God of Love instead of worshipping a god of guilt and hate.

March 24

Every act or decision we make that supports life supports *all* life, including our own. The ripples we create return to us.

March 25

Problems cannot be solved at their own calibrated level of consciousness, but only by rising to the next higher level.

March 26

What the people in the world actually want is the recognition of who they really are on the highest level, to see that the same Self radiates forth within everyone, heals their feeling of separation, and brings about a feeling of peace.

March 27

Strong intention plus dedication assisted by inspiration can surprisingly bring success, despite prior failures. This reveals the inner capacity for bravery and fortitude that greatly increases self-esteem and confidence. Many of life's travails can only be traversed by "white-knuckling it," which builds self-confidence.

March 28

All forms of loss are a confrontation to the ego and its survival mechanisms. All aspects of human life are transient, so to cling to any aspect eventually brings grief and loss. Each incident, however, is an opportunity to search within for the source of life, which is ever present, unchanging, and not subject to loss or the ravages of time.

March 29

In the state of total surrender, the body is barely perceived at all. It is only peripherally in awareness, and there is no preoccupation with it. It functions effortlessly, smoothly, and with very little attention.

March 30

This process of spirituality, in which one works through the obstacles, may seem painful at times, but it is only transitional. The mistakes now reappear and are recontextualized from a higher understanding. This process is shortened and less painful if it is realized that habitual responses are not truly personal, but are part and parcel of the inheritance of being human.

March 31

The basic purpose of spiritual work and dedication is to transcend the innate evolutionary limitations of the ego and thereby access and develop the nascent capacity of consciousness itself, which bypasses all the limitations of the ego/self. Truth then presents itself by virtue of Divine Grace. Divinity reveals Itself to those who call upon It in God's time. The pace of spiritual evolution can seem slow, but spiritual endeavor is never futile. Progress can become very sudden and very major in dimension and impact.

April 1

Humor is a means of detachment or recontextual-
izing the events of life. It is a way of being lighthearted
and "wearing the world like a loose garment." It leads to
compassion for the totality of human life and reveals the
option that one can play at life without getting involved in
it as though it were an exhausting life-and-death struggle.

April 2

The less the "wants" prevail, the greater the experience of freedom.

April 3

Spiritual devotion is a continuous inner lifestyle that incorporates constant watchful awareness. External occurrences are transitory, whereas inner qualities of consciousness are more permanent. Inner work is a constant learning process whereby there is pleasure and satisfaction in discovery and the unfolding of insight.

April 4

One must remember that love and peace are the greatest threats to the ego, which defends itself by resorting to entrenched positionalities that lie hidden in the unconscious.

April 5

To merely hear a great teaching is itself the consequence of spiritual merit. To act on it is of even greater benefit.

April 6

The person who has found inner peace can no longer be intimidated, controlled, manipulated, or programmed. In this state, one is invulnerable to the threats of the world and therefore has mastered life.

April 7

Humility is not just an attitude, but also a reality based on facts. With inner honesty, a devotee needs to realize the limitations inherent in just being human.

April 8

Do not compare yourself with others regarding "holiness," merit, goodness, deservingness, sinlessness, and so on. These are all human notions, and God is not limited by human notions.

April 9

The silent state of Awareness that underlies all movement, activity, sound, feeling, and thought is discovered to be a timeless dimension of peace.

April 10

Meaning is defined by context, which determines motive, and it is the motive that establishes spiritual value. To dedicate one's actions as a service of love to life is to sanctify them and transform them from self-seeking motives to unselfish gifts. We define excellence as dedication to the highest standards. Every act can then be held as an opportunity to glorify God by sheer purity of endeavor. All physical tasks and labor can be ingredients in one's contribution to the world. Even the smallest task can be seen as serving the common good and, if viewed in that light, work becomes ennobled.

April 11

The innate qualities of Divinity are mercy and compassion. There are no favors to be sought. It is only necessary to accept what already exists as a given.

April 12

Dedication to truth itself is the rapid road to its discovery.

April 13

All that is truly of God brings peace, harmony, and love, and is devoid of all forms of negativity. A spiritually aware person realizes that he or she can only carry the message, for it is the inner truth that is the teacher.

April 14

Looking at the feelings on the level of interpersonal relationships, we now discover another law of consciousness. Our feelings and thoughts always have an effect on other persons and affect our relationships, whether these thoughts or feelings are verbalized, expressed, or not.

April 15

Peace can be the consequence of surrender to the inevitabilities of life. The religious/spiritual skeptic can look within and observe that the inner fundamental irreducible quality of life is the capacity of awareness, consciousness, and the substrate of subjectivity.

April 16

Trust in the love, mercy, infinite wisdom, and compassion of Divinity, which sees through all human error, limitation, and frailty. Place faith and trust in the love of God, which is all-forgiving, and understand that condemnation and fear of judgment stem from the ego. Like the sun, the love of God shines equally on all. Avoid negative depictions (jealous, angry, destructive, partial, favoring, vengeful, insecure, vulnerable, contractual, and so forth) of God as an anthropomorphic projection.

April 17

Inner satisfaction becomes more important than worldly gain or the desire to control or influence others. Attraction replaces promotion. Eventually, resistance is no longer related to worldly life and its perceived values. Instead, the inner intention is one of purity and selflessness. Thus, evolution becomes the consequence of the process itself rather than a consequence of "seekingness" or acquisition.

April 18

It is obvious that higher states of consciousness have a profound effect on our relationships, because one of the laws of consciousness is *like* goes to *like*.

April 19

As the true source of happiness stems from within, desire cannot be satisfied—it is a constant projection of specialness onto the external, and is thus the pursuit of a fantasy. As one desire becomes fulfilled and satisfied, the focus then moves on to the next object of desire in an endless procession, like a carrot on a stick.

April 20

The process of creativity and genius is inherent in human consciousness. As every human has within himself the same essence of consciousness, so is genius a potential that resides within everyone. It simply waits for the right circumstance to express itself.

April 21

The goal of society in general is to succeed in the world, whereas the goal of enlightenment is to transcend beyond it.

April 22

Courage arises from commitment and integrity of alignment and dedication. A valuable characteristic of dedication is felicity, which eventually becomes empowered as a quiet but persistent inner fervor. The value of watchful witnessing is that even just awareness of an ego defect tends to undo it. By surrender and prayerful invocation, Divine Will facilitates transition from the lesser to the greater, for the Self effortlessly supports and energizes intention.

April 23

The influence that our thoughts and feelings have is, in the world's literature, called "the law of karma," or "You get what you give," or "You reap what you sow."

April 24

The world and everything in it is transitory; therefore, to cling to it brings suffering.

April 25

It is to be emphasized that that which is truly holy and of God brings only peace and love.

April 26

Conflict exists in the mind of the observer and not in that which is observed.

April 27

Be aware that your inner state is known and transmitted; the people around you will intuit what you are feeling and thinking, even if you don't verbalize it.

April 28

In reality, it is the forgiver and not the forgiven who benefits most.

April 29

By internal observation, one can differentiate that the personality is a system of learned responses and the persona is not the real "I"; the real "I" lies behind and beyond it. One is the witness of that personality, and there is no reason one has to identify with it at all.

April 30

Love is the leading edge of reality and the oneness and essence of the spirit. To deny love is to deny God.

May 1

Through surrender, we can free ourselves from being at the effect of the archetypes. The archetypes are obviously a collection of beliefs and feelings and are, therefore, programs like any other. The individual who uses the mechanism of surrender to let go of programmed beliefs and feelings has the power of choice over the archetypal patterns, rather than unconsciously being run by them.

May 2

In the reality of nonduality, there is neither privilege nor gain nor loss nor rank. Just like a cork in the sea, each spirit rises or falls to its own level in the sea of consciousness by virtue of its own choices, not by any external force or favor. Some are attracted by the light and some seek the darkness, but it all occurs of its own nature by virtue of Divine freedom and equality.

May 3

To spiritualize one's life, it is necessary only to shift one's motive. To constantly be aware of one's actual motive tends to bring up positionality and pairs of opposites, such as gain versus service or love versus greed. These then become visible and are available for spiritual work because one is now conscious of them.

May 4

The capacity to recognize the truth is a potential within human consciousness, and the combined intention of the consciousness of all people in that direction intensifies the overall field. At some intuitive level, everyone knows that truth supports life and falsity brings death.

May 5

The ego is clever. It substitutes spiritual pride for personal pride. It goes right on, undaunted. It takes personal credit for spiritual comprehension instead of realizing that the capacity for understanding itself is a spiritual gift from God.

May 6

There's a common illusion that spiritually evolved, loving people never have any negativity, as though they are already angelic. They get annoyed that they still have negative feelings, and then it's compounded by their guilt and self-frustration. They have to realize that feelings are transitory, whereas their intention to evolve remains constant.

May 7

Joy arises from within each moment of existence rather than from any outer source.

May 8

The limitations of love have to do with perceived qualities and differences. Through inner self-honesty and examination, these areas of limitation are revealed, usually as residual judgments or as the impact from prior experience. A key to making love unconditional is the willingness of forgiveness to undo past reservations or experiences, or viewing people as unlovable.

May 9

Spiritual progress is based on acceptance as a matter of free will and choice, and thus everyone experiences only the world of his or her own choosing. The universe is totally free of victims, and all eventualities are the unfolding of inner choices and decisions.

May 10

Attachment is the process whereby the suffering of loss occurs, irrespective of what the attachment is to or about: whether internal or external; whether object, relationship, social quality, or aspects of physical life. The ego perpetuates itself through its elaborate network of values, belief systems, and programs. Needs thus arise that gain more energy as they become embellished and elaborated, sometimes to the point of fixation.

May 11

The benefit of accepting one's defects instead of denying them is an increase in an inner sense of self-honesty, security, and higher self-esteem, accompanied by greatly diminished defensiveness. A self-honest person is not prone to having his or her feelings hurt by others; therefore, honest insight has an immediate benefit in the reduction of actual, as well as potential, emotional pain.

Sometimes one is more or less forced to surrender to a situation and presume that it's karmic. With spiritual research, one finds out that it is indeed karmic. Let's say you are paying off the karma of being mean to a lot of people! Now you get a chance to see what it's like to have people be mean to you. Sometimes the only reasonable thing left to do is to surrender to karmic patterns. You don't have to believe in karma as a religious doctrine in order to make this step. It's simply accepting the basic law of human interactions that "what goes around comes around," and most of us have not always been saints!

May 13

It is unrealistic as well as eventually injurious to believe that other people "should" adopt and live by one's own personal standards, morals, and code of conduct as well as interpretation of reality. Projected moralism is always expressed as "should" and often leads to resentment, hatred, grudges, or even retaliatory vengeance—and, of course, war (such as the naïve American view that all other nations "should" be democracies). One can, by choice, reject the temptation to habitual judgmentalism. The result is a great inner peace.

May 14

The way out of conflict is not to try to eliminate the negative, but instead to choose and adopt the positive. When one views that one's mission in life is to understand rather than to judge, this automatically resolves moral dilemmas.

May 15

Unconditional Love is a way of being with life that nurtures, supports, and, of its own nature, is forgiving.

May 16

Human life offers the maximum opportunity for spiritual evolution. Perception sees personal as well as social/political/ideational conflicts as obstacles to peace and happiness. In contrast, the spiritual Self sees perfection in the very same world.

May 17

The letting go of negativity and selfishness, concern for others, a heightened pleasure from their company, and higher self-esteem changes one's perspective of relationships. The capacity for lovingness increases rapidly. Much of promiscuity is an attempt to overcome unconscious fears and seek reassurance. These can all be let go of, so that more mature relationships take their place.

May 18

Complete surrender to God unveils the truth; nothing is hidden. Only the ego is blind, and Reality lies just beyond the mind. Out of the fear of becoming nothing, consciousness denies its only reality that it is everything—the infinite, everlasting Allness out of which existence itself arises.

May 19

It is only necessary to shift from devotion to the world to devotion to God and the spirit.

May 20

Realize that the depiction of God as a "judge" is a delusion of the ego that arises as a projection of guilt from the punishment of childhood. Realize that God is not a parent.

May 21

If you let go of trying to control your experience of the moment, and if you constantly surrender it like a tone of music, then you live on the crest of this exact always-ness. Experience arises like a note of music. The minute you hear a note, it's already passing away. The instant you've heard it, it's already dissolving. So every single moment is dissolving as it arises. Let go of anticipating the next moment, trying to control it, trying to hang on to the moment that has just passed. Let go clinging to what has just occurred. Let go trying to control what you think is about to occur. Then you live in an infinite space of non-time and non-event. There is an infinite peace beyond description. And you are home.

May 22

Classically, the readiness for serious spiritual work is referred to as "ripeness," at which point even hearing a single word, phrase, or name may trigger a sudden decision and commitment to truth. The advent of spiritual dedication may thus be subtle, slow, and gradual, and then take a very sudden and major jump. By whatever route, once the seed falls on ready ground, the journey begins in earnest. Commonly, the turning point can be triggered by an unexpected flash of insight, and from that moment on, life changes.

May 23

The Self is like a person's inner grandmother who watches over him so he does not forget to take his raincoat or mail the rent check. God is not ominous but loving; fear arises from the imagination.

May 24

Within limits, we tend to experience the reflection of what we have become.

May 25

A helpful source of strength during the processing out of painful emotions is to identify with all humanity and realize that suffering is universal and innate to the phenomenon of being human and the evolution of the ego.

May 26

In truth, we exist and survive, not because of the ego, but in spite of it.

May 27

We change the world not by what we say or do, but as a consequence of what we have become. Thus, every spiritual aspirant serves the world.

May 28

We honor that which we esteem in others as well as ourselves. Out of this, one honors one's own humanity and that of others and ends up honoring all of life in all its expressions by resignation to Divine Will. With surrender of the ego, the spirit becomes aware of the sanctity of existence.

May 29

Life unfolds of its own and does not need commentary. The habit of editorializing about what is witnessed needs to be voluntarily surrendered to God.

May 30

It is helpful to remember that neither truth nor enlightenment is something to be found, sought, acquired, gained, or possessed. The Infinite Presence is always present, and its realization occurs of itself when the obstacles to that realization are removed. It is, therefore, not necessary to study the truth, but only to let go of that which is fallacious. Moving away the clouds does not cause the sun to shine, but merely reveals what was hidden all along.

May 31

There is a peaceful relief when judgment and criticism are abandoned, since they cause constant unconscious guilt as well as fear of retribution.

June 1

Awareness of the overall silent contextual field is facilitated by a contemplative lifestyle that could be likened to shifting interest from details to "the big picture." It "gets" overall qualities of atmosphere without going into specifics, and therefore intuits generalities rather than thinking or analyzing.

The resistance of the ego/mind is that it is afraid it might "miss" something, as it is addicted to processing the details of the content of form, which is the attraction and lure of the world. To "renounce the world" means to withdraw energy from it and decline activities that require attention to specifics, thereby abiding in the Self rather than in the amusements of the self.

June 2

Just one instant in a very high state can completely change a person's orientation to life, as well as his goals and values. It can be said that the individual who was is no more, and a new person is born out of the experience. Through hard-won progress on a dedicated spiritual path, this is the very mechanism of spiritual evolution.

June 3

Spiritual evolution occurs as the result of removing obstacles and not actually acquiring anything new. Devotion enables surrender of the mind's vanities and cherished illusions so that the mind progressively becomes more free and open to the light of Truth.

June 4

Wallowing in guilt is feeding the ego and is an indulgence. Therefore, there has to be the willingness to surrender it.

June 5

Putting one's survival on something outside oneself therefore results in states of powerlessness, victimhood, and weakness by virtue of having projected the source of one's power outside of oneself.

June 6

As spiritual awareness advances, the flow of spiritual energy increases and enables transcending prior, seemingly insurmountable obstacles. As the attractions of the world and emotions decrease, there is a progressive attraction to qualities such as beauty, lovability, and peace, rather than "things" or seeming gains. Forgiveness becomes a habitual attitude, and the innate innocence of all creation shines forth. The teachings of great saints and teachers become one's own from within.

June 7

Out of all-inclusive, unconditional compassion comes the healing of all mankind.

June 8

Our experience of the world and life is totally the result of inner beliefs and positionalities. Out of love and respect for God arises the willingness to surrender all these prejudgments, and the humility that ensues opens the doors to the splendor of reality, which is the revelation of the Self. Love is the magic catalyst that brings about the awareness. In the end, faith is replaced by certainty, and therefore it is said that God is found by those who seek Him.

June 9

Like matter and energy, life cannot be destroyed but can only change form. Thus, death is actually only the leaving of the body. The sense of identity is, however, unbroken. The state of "me" (self) is constant and continues after it separates from the physical expiration; that is, there has to be a "who" that goes on to heaven or other realms or chooses to reincarnate.

June 10

Failure to internalize goals leads to frustration and resentment.

June 11

How best to "serve the highest good" is in accordance with the prevailing level of consciousness of the observer. There is no single answer for everyone.

June 12

Life itself has no opinion; it just is. Life effortlessly diverts quickly from one form to another without innate reaction or resistance. It does not even register a reaction to change of form. Life, like light, is innately formless and beyond preference, resistance, or reaction.

June 13

To align one's life with spiritual intention expands its meaning and significance. While the ego/body/mind's life span is limited and temporary, the life of the spirit is eternal, and its importance thus eclipses transitory gains of ego satisfaction. The lesser is then surrendered to the greater by alignment, commitment, and agreement—because it is freely chosen rather than imposed, there is a lessening of resistance.

June 14

When the mind stops talking, one *is* aware that one is life. One is immersed in it rather than being on the surface, talking about it. Paradoxically, this enables full participation. When egocentricity diminishes, the joy of freedom and the sheer flow of life sweep one into total surrender. One then stops reacting to life, so it can be enjoyed with serenity.

June 15

Imperfection exists only in the mind's thoughts. No imperfection exists in the world as it is.

June 16

A question cannot be asked unless there is already the potentiality of the answer.

June 17

By being loving toward others, we discover that we are surrounded by love and lovingness. When we unreservedly support life without expecting gain, life supports us in return. Whenever we abandon gain as a motive, life responds with unexpected generosity. And when we perceive in this way, the miraculous begins to appear in the life of every dedicated spiritual aspirant.

June 18

When people admit they are powerless over something, instead of going weak with the muscle test, they suddenly go strong.

June 19

Without consciousness, we would not "know" or even "know if we know," so that consciousness is the determinable awareness of existence, irrespective of the content of that existence. Thus, consciousness itself can be accepted as an obvious reality, without the elaboration of being Divine (as recommended by the Buddha). To "be" is one thing; to know that one "is" obviously requires a more transcendent quality.

June 20

I, of myself, really know nothing is factual, for at best, the mind has only impressions and presumptions. Life "makes sense" solely in retrospect.

June 21

Selecting a basic spiritual dictum to live by operationally becomes a set of attitudes that change perception. It is a style of positioning oneself and relating to life rather than a set of linear belief systems. Attitudes tend to generalize as discernment rather than definable perception.

June 22

The difficulty with a closed mind is that it is innately prideful.

June 23

Transformation has to do with the person's re-owning that they are the source of their own happiness, and that the power is within them.

June 24

To become more conscious is the greatest gift anyone can give to the world; moreover, in a ripple effect, the gift comes back to its source.

June 25

One has to see through the mind's illusion that it knows anything. This is called "humility" and has the value of opening the door for realizations, revelations, and intuitive knowingness.

June 26

Appearance is not essence, perception is not reality, and the cover is not the book. Error is quite often convincing, which is an unpleasant fact to consider and accept. Everyone secretly believes that his or her own personal view of the world is real, factual, and true.

June 27

The presence of God as love is self-revealing, since the duality of perception ceases as a consequence of surrendering positionalities. Love is therefore the doorway between the linear and the nonlinear domains. It is the grand avenue to the discovery of God.

June 28

Divinity knows its own; therefore, to accept that truth is to already feel joy. To not experience joy by understanding this means that it is being resisted.

June 29

Q: What is the most serviceable presumptive view of the world for a spiritual student/devotee/seeker?

A: Presume that the world's actual "purpose" is perfect and fully known only by God. See it as neutral overall, but with the benefit that it provides optimal opportunity for spiritual growth and the evolution of consciousness. It is a school for enlightenment and the revelation of Divinity, whereby consciousness/awareness reawakens to its source. Thus, to pursue enlightenment in and of itself serves the world and God.

June 30

Energy fields are so powerful that they dominate our perception. They are really portals out of which we see the world. We often hear that this is really just a world of mirrors, and that all we experience is our own energy field reflected back upon us as perception and experiencing.

July 1

Q: What characteristics facilitate comprehension and transformation?

A: Dedication, devotion, faith, prayer, surrender, and inspiration. When the barriers are relinquished, Truth reveals itself spontaneously.

July 2

The realization that there is a source of joy and happiness that is beyond the ego is a major step. Then curiosity and an interest in how to reach spiritual goals arises. Belief also arises, which is then bolstered by faith, and eventually by experience. Next follows the acquisition of instruction, information, and the practice of what has been learned. By invitation, the spiritual energy increases, followed by dedication and the willingness to surrender all obstacles.

July 3

What the world ignores as a weed is of beauty equal to that of the flower. The living-sculpture design of all nature is equal, without classification, and everything is realized to be of the same merit or worth. All is an expression of Divinity as creation—all is equally sacred and holy.

July 4

There is absolutely nothing in ordinary human experience to compare with the joy of the presence of the love of God. No sacrifice is too great nor effort too much in order to realize that presence.

July 5

The truly successful have no inclination to act arrogantly, for they consider themselves not better than others, just more fortunate. They see their position as a *stewardship*, a responsibility to exercise their influence for the greatest benefit of all.

July 6

Our own energy field is coloring everything else.

July 7

Spiritual reality is a greater source of pleasure and satisfaction than the world can supply. It is endless and always available in the present instead of the future. It is actually more exciting because one learns to live on the crest of the current moment, instead of on the back of the wave (which is the past) or on the front of the wave (which is the future). There is greater freedom from living on the exciting knife-edge of the moment than being a prisoner of the past or having expectations of the future.

July 8

Everyone already at a certain level knows that they "are"—the ego then quibbles about the details of definition, but the Self is not fooled by the ruse. All false identifications can be dropped in an instant with the willingness to surrender all mental activities to God.

July 9

The ego gets a grim pleasure and satisfaction from suffering and all the dishonest levels of pride, anger, desire, guilt, shame, and grief. The secret pleasure of suffering is addictive. Many people devote their entire lives to it and encourage others to follow suit. To stop this mechanism, the pleasure of the payoff has to be identified and willingly surrendered to God. Out of shame, the ego blocks out conscious awareness of its machinations, especially the secretiveness of the game of "victim."

July 10

In this interconnected universe, every improvement we make in our private world improves the world at large for everyone. We all float on the collective level of consciousness of mankind so that any increment we add comes back to us. We all add to our common buoyancy by our efforts to benefit life. What we do to serve life automatically benefits all of us because we are all included in that which is life. We *are* life. It's a scientific fact that "what is good for you is good for me."

July 11

By committing to inner honesty, it will become apparent that the underpinning of the ego's responses is the pleasure that is derived from them. There is an inner satisfaction that is the payoff of self-pity, anger, rage, hate, pride, guilt, fear, and the like. This inner pleasure, as morbid as it may sound, energizes and propagates all these emotions. To undo their influence, it is merely necessary to be willing to forego and surrender these questionable, inner secret pleasures to God and to look to God only for joy and happiness.

July 12

To undo shame, it is helpful to realize that it is based on pride. The loss of status is painful to the degree that the ego relies on pride as a prop to self-esteem. Were it not for narcissistic pride, a mistake or negative feedback would be experienced only as a regret and ascribed to human frailty and fallibility. Mistakes help one retain humility.

July 13

Surrender is a constant process of not resisting or clinging to the moment, but instead, continuously turning it over to God. The attention is thus focused on the process of letting go and not on the content of the "what" that is being surrendered.

July 14

The purpose of the Map of Consciousness is to create a context from which to view and experience the world and see that it presents whole new avenues that begin to open up automatically.

July 15

In and of itself, anger is merely a subjective emotion that does not actually accomplish anything in the world, as the use of reason and restraint would. Anger is used by the ego as a substitute for courage, which really only requires being resolute, determined, or committed.

July 16

To endeavor to evolve spiritually is the greatest gift one can give. It actually uplifts all mankind from within because of the nature of power itself. Power radiates and is shared, whereas force is limited, self-defeating, and evanescent. All society is subliminally and subtly influenced by every kind and loving thought, word, or deed.

July 17

The ego clings to emotionality, which is intimately connected with its positionalities; it pretends to think that it has no other choices. To "surrender to God" means to stop looking to the ego for solace and thrills and to discover the endless, serene joy of peace. To look within is to find the underlying, ever-present source of the illumination of the mind itself.

July 18

Our first really major secret is to reverse the world's understanding of cause and effect. Cause, which is power, is "in here." What we see "out there" is merely the consequence. It is automatic. It can't help but happen because of the universal laws of life. The world envies the wrong thing when it envies the consequence. It tries to imitate, but doesn't know *what* to imitate. For it to work in our own lives we have to imitate the cause, not the effect.

July 19

The events of the world trigger responses based on perceptions. It is a great theater that invites expressions of perceptions, illusions, and projections of positionalities. One can either turn off the television and avoid it or see it as a major teaching tool.

July 20

The will is activated and empowered by devotion, and it responds with inspiration, which leads to illumination by grace. The personal will dissolves into Divine Will, and the spark that leads to the spiritual search and inquiry is a Divine gift.

July 21

The spiritually evolved person who has few wants or attachments is relatively immune to grief, as the experience of the source of happiness originates from within and is not dependent on externals. If the source of happiness is acquired through ego mechanisms, it is based on imagery, belief systems, and projected values rather than on Absolute Reality itself, which is invulnerable to loss. Objects, qualities, or relationships become overvalued by virtue of the mechanism of attachment and the ensuing projection of value.

July 22

Devotion dissolves fear, doubt, and hesitation; and it clarifies uncertainty. Intention also becomes even stronger, as does trust in God. Then arises the inner decision to totally abandon oneself to God.

July 23

The spirit and the heart are one. It is the heart that is at one with God, not the mind. To discover one's own heart is to discover God.

July 24

One can ask oneself the question, *Is this worth giving up God for?* Thus, ego positionality has a price, which is where the willingness should be addressed. Each positionality is based on the presumption that its fulfillment will bring happiness. Thus, nothing is really valued aside from the illusion that it will bring that about.

July 25

Success comes about automatically from knowing where to look. Not *what* to look for, but *where* to look. We do not look at what we have, nor at what we do, but at what we are. Once we find within ourselves what we've been searching for, we won't have to bother looking "out there."

July 26

The human world represents a purgatorial-like range of opportunities and choices, from the most grim to the exalted, from criminality to nobility, from fear to courage, from despair to hope, and from greed to charity. Thus, if the purpose of the human experience is to evolve, then this world is perfect just as it is.

July 27

We cannot allow the mind to come up with a belief system without challenging it. If the mind unconsciously has been working against us, and we have been unaware of how much power it has, we can turn it around and use that power on our own behalf. The same power that undid us can now work for us when we consciously utilize the power of mind.

July 28

The energy field of love is innately gratifying in and of its own quality. It is discovered that love is available everywhere and that lovingness results in the return of love. Although love may start out as conditional, with spiritual intention it becomes a way of life and a way of relating to life in all its expressions.

July 29

What the ego cannot lift with all its might is like a feather to the grace of God.

July 30

Look at what we used to think of as enemies and competitors as merely sources of inspiration. What they're challenging is within us—not us against them.

July 31

True asceticism is simply a matter of economy of effort. It is not possessions themselves but the presumed importance or value projected onto them that is significant. Therefore, it is recommended that one "wear the world like a loose garment."

August 1

Effective spiritual endeavor is a consequence of constancy and persistence rather than fits and starts of enthusiasm.

August 2

The source of happiness is within, and it is released under favorable circumstances when the mind experiences a desired outcome. Through inner examination, one will discover that the event merely triggers an innate capacity. With the discovery that the source of happiness is actually within one's inner self and therefore cannot be lost, there is a reduction of fear.

August 3

An extremely valuable insight that is learned by all spiritually evolved persons in the course of their development is seeing one's own personal consciousness as the decisive influence that determines all that occurs in one's life.

August 4

Truly successful people know that the purchaser of their services, whatever they are—be they entertaining, singing, dancing, engineering, whatever—is always the same customer. *There is only one customer in this whole world.* The name of that customer is "human nature."

August 5

To know that the Self is context—and, in contrast, the self is content—is already a huge leap forward. The naïve seeker merely keeps reshuffling the content.

August 6

If the goal of life is to do the very best one can do at each unfolding moment of existence, then, through spiritual work, one has already escaped the primary cause of suffering. In the stop-frame of the radical present, there is no life story to react to or edit. With this "one-pointedness" of mind, it soon becomes obvious that everything merely "is as it is," without comment or adjectives.

August 7

To surrender a goal does not mean to automatically lose it. What is illusive via greed often effortlessly materializes as a consequence of evolving to a higher level of consciousness.

August 8

Accept that the concept of "the fear of God" is ignorance. God is peace and love, and nothing else.

August 9

Those attitudes of generosity, caring, bigness, creativity, resourcefulness, and adaptability are all automatically rising out of the fact that the one directing the enterprise has human nature. These are qualities of human nature itself; therefore, they exist in all of us.

August 10

Fears are eliminated by graceful acceptance of the qualities inherent in the human condition, which brings to awareness the comforting realization that one's discomforts are shared equally by all. This results in a healing compassion toward all life. To become loving brings an end to the fear of loss of love, for lovingness engenders love wherever it goes.

August 11

Inner peace results from surrender of either attractions or aversions. Perceived values are primarily projections of "wants" and "not wants." The fewer the "wants," the greater the ease and satisfaction of life.

August 12

What needs to be surrendered are not the objects of desire, but the quality of desiring and the imbuing of the objects with the magical inflation of value.

August 13

In true spiritual endeavor, no actual sacrifices are necessary or expected. *Sacrifice* in ordinary terminology means loss or even painful loss. True sacrifice really means the letting go of the lesser for the greater and is self-rewarding rather than depleting.

August 14

Each time a new goal is set, it is set from the experience of we don't have it and we want it. Then what happens is either we get it or we don't. If we don't get it, we say we're unhappy. If we do get it, we say we're satisfied. If our goal is limited, the success will be limited.

August 15

As the payoffs of the ego are refused and surrendered, its grip on the psyche lessens, and spiritual experience progresses as the residuals of doubt are progressively relinquished. As a consequence, belief is replaced by experiential knowledge; the depth and intensity of devotion increases and may eventually supersede and eclipse all other worldly activities and interests.

August 16

Rational humility, through which the mind becomes teachable, is basic to learning. The mind can then absorb, incorporate, and identify with verifiable and true knowledge. The key to success is to study and imitate a truthful authority rather than resist or attack it through competitive envy, jealousy, or hostility.

August 17

All the mind's statements are provisional at best, and an awareness of that limitation is an intrinsic quality of wisdom. Wisdom denotes a degree of humility as well as flexibility. It also implies a conservative, cautious attitude that is aware that further information will accrue over time and experience. Thus, wisdom considers all knowledge to be provisional and subject to change, not only in meaning but also in significance and value.

August 18

The primary defect now is, as it always has been, that the design of the human mind renders it intrinsically incapable of being able to tell truth from falsehood. This single, most crucial of all inherited defects lies at the root of all human distress and calamity.

August 19

The Self is like a magnetic attraction by which the personal will is progressively surrendered and resistance is weakened. Thus, the pathway itself is self-fulfilling and gratifying, and reveals progressive rewards. Each step, no matter how seemingly small, is equally valuable.

August 20

The major limitation of consciousness is its innocence. Consciousness is gullible; it believes everything it hears. Consciousness is like hardware that will play back any software that's put into it. We never lose the innocence of our own consciousness; it persists, naïve and trusting, like an impressionable child. Its only guardian is a discerning awareness that scrutinizes the incoming program.

August 21

Spiritual evolution is a lifetime commitment and a way of life by which the world and all experience subserve spiritual intention. There is no greater calling than to choose to be a servant of God. With spiritual progress, each increment is of equal importance—for, analogously, it is only through the removal of a single brick that an entire wall collapses, and the seemingly impossible becomes possible.

August 22

We see that success comes automatically to people because of their presence. All of these people, we will notice, seem to have the guts and the self-assurance to just be who they are. They capitalize on what to other people would have been limitations. As we said, facts are not what carry power. Rather, it is our attitudes about them.

August 23

Make a gift of your life and lift all mankind by being kind, considerate, forgiving, and compassionate at all times, in all places, and under all conditions, with everyone as well as yourself. That is the greatest gift anyone can give.

August 24

Everyone has the opportunity to contribute to harmony and beauty by kindness to others and thereby support the human spirit. That which is freely given to life flows back to us because we are equally part of that life. Like ripples on the water, every gift returns to the giver. What we affirm in others, we actually affirm in ourselves.

August 25

Q: Is the ego the source of karma?

A: It is its locus and repository. It is very important to realize that the ego and karma are one and the same thing.

August 26

Spiritual progress ensues automatically from choosing goodwill, forgiveness, and lovingness as a way of being in the world at large rather than viewing it as a gain-seeking transaction.

August 27

Freedom is the opportunity to fashion one's own destiny and learn the inherent spiritual truths that are essential. For merit or demerit to occur, the choices have to be made in a state of belief and experience to be considered "real." Thus, even illusion subserves spiritual growth, for it seems real at the time.

August 28

Success, therefore, is only success when it is shared. The restaurant owner shares the joy and the delight of his success. The chef comes out and displays the joy and delight of his creation, which is obviously for the customers' joy and delight as well. The whole place abounds in goodwill. Everyone has it made in this experience. What's crucial is that the customers also have it made in experiencing the owner and chef's enterprise. Pleasing people is a matter of knowing genuinely what they enjoy.

August 29

Awareness is a quality of consciousness itself that is not encumbered by having to "do" anything. It just "is," and by virtue of its innate capacity, apprehends essence directly. The presence of Divinity as Self is effortless.

August 30

Temptation, seduction, desirability, and allure are all projections having to do with appearance and presumptions. These are associated with programmed fantasies of gain. Satisfaction of projected values constitutes the world of illusion.

August 31

We witness, observe, and record apparent processions of experience. But even in awareness itself, nothing actually happens. Awareness merely registers what is being experienced; it has no effect on it. Awareness is the all-encompassing attractor field of unlimited power identical with life itself. *And there is nothing the mind believes that is not erroneous at a higher level of awareness.*

September 1

When someone is good at what they do, they become the true people pleaser. We are all extremely pleased with excellence, with a great performance. What pleases us about a great performer is the heart involved. It is the heart of the champion. We applaud their creativity. We congratulate their enterprise. We praise their commitment to excellence. We commend the way they hold themselves in front of us, as well as the way they hold themselves to themselves. What made Luciano Pavarotti great was not just his voice, as there have been a lot of magnificent Italian tenors in the world. He had the true humility of the great. Genuine people pleasing is not catering; it's manifesting excellence.

September 2

The mind is caught between desires and aversions, both of which are binding. An aversion is also innately an attachment to a conditional perception, and it is disassembled by acceptance.

September 3

Spiritual evolution is the automatic consequence of watching the mind—and its proclivities as an "it"—from the general viewpoint of the paradigm of context rather than content. Instead of trying to force change, it is merely necessary to allow Divinity to do so by deeply surrendering all control, resistance, and illusions of gain or loss. It is not necessary to destroy or attack illusions but merely to allow them to fall away.

September 4

Cessation of fear is the result of learning that the source of happiness is within. It stems from recognizing that this source is the joy of one's own existence, which is continuous and not dependent on externals. This results from surrendering expectations and demands on one's self, the world, and others. The thought *I can only be happy if I win or get what I want* is a guarantee of worry, anxiety, and unhappiness.

September 5

Spiritual progress occurs in stages: In the beginning, one learns of spiritual realities and studies them. Then comes the practice and application of the teachings in every aspect of life, and eventually one becomes the prayer. Through devotion, commitment, and practice, spiritual concepts become experiential realities.

September 6

Spiritual teachings need to be accepted to become integrated. Resistance comes from the ego, which lacks humility and which, out of pride, resents being "wrong." It is better to realize that one is not giving up wrong views but is instead adopting better ones.

September 7

Malice literally makes us sick; we are always the victims of our own vindictiveness. Even secret hostile thoughts result in a physiological attack on one's own body.

September 8

Like any enterprise, success comes from not only knowing what to do, but knowing what *not* to do. Understanding what not to do comes out of understanding the principles of what *to* do. Really blowing it is one example of an opportunity out of which we can make lemonade out of lemons. The purpose is to analyze a mistake in such a way that it serves us, so we can come out the better for it. It is also important that we resolve all regret and bitterness and find a silver lining in the cloud.

September 9

Realization is not a "gain" or an accomplishment, nor is it something that is "given" as a reward for being good. These are all notions from childhood. God is immutable and cannot be manipulated into granting favors or seduced by bargaining or adulation. Worship benefits the worshipper by reinforcing commitment and inspiration. God is still, silent, and unmoving.

September 10

The narcissistic core of the ego is aligned with being "right," whether being "right" means being in agreement with wisdom or rejecting it as invalid. With humility, the serious searcher discovers that the mind alone, despite its education, is unable to resolve the dilemma of how to ascertain and validate truth, which would require confirmation by subjective experience as well as objective, provable criteria.

September 11

Disruption of life by the unexpected also creates anxiety at the forced readjustment, which may require major decision making. It is important to know that spiritual research indicates that all suffering and emotional pain result from resistance. Its cure is via surrender and acceptance, which relieve the pain.

September 12

Courage does not mean absence of fear, but the willingness to surmount it—which, when accomplished, reveals hidden strength and the capacity for fortitude. Fear of failure is diminished by realizing that one is responsible for the intention and effort but not the result, which is dependent on many other conditions and factors that are nonpersonal.

September 13

When the goodwill is gone, success is gone. When the goodwill is gone, trust, faith, satisfaction, attitude, customer loyalty, and all that makes life worthwhile go with it. It all goes down the tubes together.

September 14

Q: *Where does one begin the search for spiritual truth, Self-realization, and Enlightenment?*

A: It is simple. Begin with who and what you are. All truth is found within. Use verified teachings as a guide.

September 15

Spiritual learning does not occur in a linear progression like logic. It is more that familiarity with spiritual principles and disciplines opens awareness and self-realization. Nothing "new" is learned; instead, what already exists presents itself as completely obvious.

September 16

As evolution expresses itself in gradations, some people will be farther along the road than others. When we see this simple fact, forgiveness and compassion replace anger, fear, hatred, or condemnation. The willingness to forgive others is reflected in our own capacity for self-forgiveness and acceptance.

September 17

Simple kindness to one's self and all that lives is the most powerful transformational force of all. It produces no backlash, has no downside, and never leads to loss or despair. It increases one's own true power without exacting any toll. But to reach maximum power, such kindness can permit *no* exceptions, nor can it be practiced with the expectation of some selfish reward. And its effect is as far-reaching as it is subtle.

September 18

To consciously choose alignment with Divinity and truth is reempowering and shifts identity from the self to the Self, resulting in an increase in confidence, courage, and personal dignity rather than self-abasement or self-denigration. Total surrender brings peace; partial or conditional surrender bring lingering doubt.

September 19

If we're not coming from being a friend of life and a friend of human nature, there's no guarantee the world is going to be our friend either.

September 20

Partial and limited positionalities create the illusions called "problems." In reality, no such thing as a problem is possible; there is merely what we want and what we don't want. Suffering is due to resistance.

September 21

When life loses meaning, we first go into depression; when life becomes sufficiently meaningless, we leave it altogether. Force has transient goals; when those goals are reached, the emptiness of meaninglessness remains. Power, on the other hand, motivates us endlessly. If our lives are dedicated, for instance, to enhancing the welfare of everyone we contact, our lives can never lose meaning.

September 22

The absolute subjectivity of revealed truth precludes all considerations or uncertainties, which stem only from the ego. When the ego collapses, all argument ceases and is replaced by silence. Doubt *is* the ego.

September 23

Dedication is a more important sign of integrity than enthusiasm. It is necessary to have faith in a pathway and clear away doubts to ascertain if they are realistic or merely forms of resistance. A seeker should have the security and support of inner certainty and firm conviction that are consequent to study, personal research, and investigation. Thus, a pathway should be intrinsically reconfirming by discovery and inner experience. A true pathway unfolds, is self-revelatory, and is subject to reconfirmation experientially.

September 24

The source of resistance to spiritual endeavor is the narcissistic core of the ego itself, which secretly claims sovereignty and authorship of one's existence, decisions, and actions. Thus, despite one's best efforts, willfulness and desire for gain or control have continued to erupt repetitiously.

This pattern can be diminished simply by accepting that it is natural for the ego to be vain, greedy, hateful, prideful, resentful, envious, and more. These were learned accretions to the ego during its evolutionary development over eons of time. Therefore, it is not necessary to feel guilty because these primitive emotions merely need to be outgrown and discarded in the transition from self-interest to Self-interest.

September 25

The guarantee of success is the inner knowing that it was the consequence of your awareness of some inner truth of human nature that doesn't belong to you as an individual. It gives you the humility you need to withstand the assaults of success. A real test it is . . . one of the biggest tests in the world. Don't let your ego spoil and exploit that which was the very source of your charm.

Gratitude is one of the best defenses. If you've discovered your gift and now it is bringing home the bacon, then be grateful for it. Be thankful and seek to share the success with others rather than to show it off pridefully.

September 26

The downside of pride is arrogance and denial. These characteristics block growth.

September 27

The source of pain is not the belief system itself but one's attachment to it and the inflation of its imaginary value. The inner processing of attachments is dependent on the exercise of the will, which alone has the power to undo the mechanism of attachment by the process of surrender. This may be subjectively experienced or contextualized as sacrifice, although it is actually a liberation. The emotional pain of loss arises from the attachment itself and not from the "what" that has been lost.

September 28

True happiness is always in the "right now" of this moment. The ego is always anticipating completion and satisfaction in the future "when" a desire gets fulfilled.

September 29

Spiritual purity is the consequence of self-honesty, which is a result of true devotion. To be a servant of God is to align with Divine guidance, which leads to looking to the Self rather than catering to the self or the world.

September 30

Q: How should one envision spiritual work?

A: The process is one of discovery and is thus directed within. It is by influence of the Self that spiritual endeavor becomes chosen as a life goal. It is primarily a decision.

October 1

People with adequate self-esteem have no need to hate others.

October 2

Nothing in the world of form is permanent. Eventually, all has to be surrendered to the will of God. To succeed at surrendering, it is necessary to realize that God's will is not personalized to suit individual wishes. The will of God is really the karmic design of the entire universe. To surrender to God's will is to surrender to the truth that nothing other than the Ultimate Reality is permanent.

October 3

When we blow it, one way to recapture what we had going for us is through absolute honesty. The reestablishment of our integrity and credibility is accomplished by openly admitting a mistake when we make one. As a result of that, we demonstrate to the world a genuine change of heart. The world will forgive us . . . Everyone's made mistakes. Mistakes are not the cause of failure—they are merely springboards defining what was out of alignment, correcting it, and coming through it at a higher level. We come out either a loser or a champion, depending on how we handled the mistake.

October 4

All fields of human knowledge change over time, and even the reporting of history itself is subject to revision based on new discoveries and methodologies. Thus, all beliefs and information are tentative in that even if the facts don't change, their significance or meaning is subject to change over time.

October 5

Satisfaction and a feeling of success can be complete and total without anything at all happening "out there." That's what I mean by transcending the world, by no longer being dependent on the effect of it and the victim of "out there." Successful people have so many areas of satisfaction in their lives that they don't have any areas of vulnerability. Thus, if the expected result does not occur, they don't go into an emotional reaction about it.

October 6

That which manifests and is then said to exist is knowable by virtue of awareness alone, which is that quality of consciousness that allows the knowledge, experience, and awareness that one exists or that one *is*. To *be* is one thing, but to *know that you are* is another.

October 7

To the spiritual aspirant, desire and attachments are deterrents to progress, and as they arise, what they symbolize can be surrendered to God.

October 8

The wise know that the intellect can take one only so far, and beyond that, faith and belief must substitute for knowledge.

October 9

God's grace could be understood as the absolute certainty of the karmic coherence of the entire universe in all its expressions as realms and possibilities. Grace is the provision within the realm of consciousness for the availability to use all the means to salvation and absolute freedom. By choice, one determines one's own fate. There are no arbitrary forces to be reckoned with.

October 10

Humility removes the ego's underpinnings of judgmentalism, positionality, and moralizing.

October 11

The average person's psyche is overwhelmed by layers of programmed belief systems of which they are unaware. Out of naïveté and the belief in the principles of causality, the supposed causes and their solutions are sought "out there." With maturity and the wisdom of spirituality, the search becomes directed inwardly, where the source and resolution are finally discovered.

October 12

True strength and power comes from the ability to stick by one's principles no matter what . . . The rule is: no compromise with that which benefits and supports the lives of everyone, that which inspires, that which uplifts, that which validates, and that which honors life. Success comes from understanding the nature of life. Once it is comprehended, nothing but success is possible. This doesn't mean that struggle may not ensue; in overcoming old ways of being and adopting new ones, there may indeed be a period of struggle.

October 13

Personal judgment is based on perception that is reinforced by belief and prior programming, all of which are held in place by the payoff of the negative energies of the ego. The ego just "loves" suffering a "wrong," being the martyr, being misunderstood, and being the endless victim of life's vicissitudes. Consequently, it gets an enormous payoff—not only from the positionality itself but also from sympathy, self-pity, entitlements, importance, or being "center stage" in which the self is the hero or heroine of the melodrama.

October 14

To transcend the world requires compassion and acceptance, the result of inner humility, by which the world is surrendered to God with increased peace of mind.

October 15

Supplication and prayer to Divinity are facilitated by a profound and deep surrender to humility. This humility is merely the truthful acknowledgment of the actual fact that the ego/mind, by virtue of its structure and design, is intrinsically incapable of being able to differentiate truth from falsehood (that is, essence from appearance).

October 16

What is searching for higher truth is not a personal "I" but an aspect of consciousness itself, which expresses as inspiration, devotion, dedication, and perseverance—all of which are aspects of the spiritual will. Therefore, the source of the search for the Self is the Self itself actualizing the necessary processes by virtue of its own qualities, which are facilitated by Grace.

October 17

In a universe where "like goes to like" and "birds of a feather fly together," we attract to us that which we emanate.

October 18

Q: *The attractions of the world seem endless. Is it really safe to go there? I often just want to escape.*

A: The attractions are not innate to the world, but reflect projected values and the expectation of the payoffs of ego satisfactions. In actuality, joy stems from within and is not dependent on externals. Pleasure is associated with what is valued and esteemed. Much of projected value arises from imagination, and values reflect desires. In reality, nothing is more valuable than anything else other than spiritual fulfillment.

October 19

All things are self-created by Divine expression as existence. Therefore, each "thing" can only be what it is because of the totality of the entire universe.

October 20

If our purpose is to make this a better world to live in for everyone or to increase the safety, joy, and beauty of life, then everyone can subscribe to that. Coming from a universal principle is coming from power. Coming from self-interest is coming from force.

October 21

Truth prevails when falsity is surrendered. To do this, however, requires great dedication, courage, and faith, which are supplied by Divine inspiration in response to surrender. The trigger is the consent of Divine Will.

October 22

An analysis of the nature of consciousness reveals that redemption occurs as the result of the return of consciousness to its original pristine state of nonduality. It can do so only by the "obedience" of surrendering the dualities of will and willfulness of the ego to the nonduality of God's Truth. The return from the duality of the ego to the nonduality of the spirit is so difficult and unlikely that only by Divine Grace is it even possible. Thus, man needs a savior to be his advocate, his inspiration, and the fulcrum of his salvation from the pain and suffering of the ego.

October 23

Simply stated, integrity is strong, "works," and is constructive and successful, whereas its opposite fails. Integrity is therefore practical; its absence leads to weakness and collapse.

October 24

Traditionally, the relinquishment of the ego's programs has been described as arduous and difficult, requiring many lifetimes to accomplish. On the contrary, a profound humility and the willingness to surrender all to God at great depth make it possible for the transition to occur in a split second. Thus, the pathway to enlightenment may be viewed as a slow process or a sudden one.

October 25

The most important quality necessary for true growth and evolution is the practice and principle of humility. It is far less painful to voluntarily adopt a fundamental attitude of humility than to have it thrust upon oneself as the painful consequence of ineptitude. Despite its negative public and social image in some quarters of society, humility is indicative of expertise, wisdom, and maturity. Because truth is the very bedrock and ultimate reality upon which humility is based, it is not a vulnerability in and of itself. Rather, humility reveals that the mind can only "know about," and that it cannot differentiate between appearance and essence.

October 26

Q: How can one prevent the development of a spiritual ego? Each success seems like it would feed it.

A: Realize that there is no such entity as the doer of deeds or actions. There is no doer/self to take blame or credit. Progress is the result of a quality of consciousness that has been activated by the assent of the spiritual will. Spiritual inspiration becomes the energy that is operating; it doesn't emanate from the ego/self.

October 27

As the ego's dominance of perception recedes, so does the appearance of the world and the mind's interpretations. Decisions are based on projected perceptions. Thus, the mind perceives endless illusions, including classifications based on judgments. Those that are interpreted as "good" options are attractive to choice and agreement. Therefore, all perceptions reflect content.

October 28

We cannot become strong by catering to human weakness. We become strong by supporting strength. We become dynamic when we support the aliveness of others. We become great when we support the greatness of others. We become beautiful when we support the beauty of life. If we are truly coming from the heart, we don't have to worry about success. The world will love us, be loyal to us, support us, and forgive us all kinds of mistakes. If we treat all of our customers like royalty, surprisingly we will find ourselves living a rather royal life.

October 29

One's range of choice is ordinarily limited only by one's vision.

October 30

The true source of joy and happiness is the realization of one's existence in this very moment. The source of pleasure always comes from within, even though it is occasioned by some external event or acquisition. In any one instant of time, no such thing as a problem can exist. Unhappiness arises from going beyond the reality of the now and creating a story out of the past or the future—which, because neither exists, has no reality.

October 31

Fear itself actually precludes the awareness of the presence of God. Only when it is abandoned does profound surrender of the resistant ego reveal a peace beyond understanding.

November 1

In gratitude for the gift of life, one dedicates that life back as a gift to God through selfless service to His creation as all of life.

November 2

One "owes" contrition and confession only to the Self. One "owes" the undoing of "sin and guilt" to the Self. One "owes" the obligation to change one's ways to the Self. One "owes" it to the Self to give up positionalities. Suffering only serves the ego. Of what use would it be to God, Who has no needs or emotion, and Who would in no way be pleasured by human agony?

November 3

There is no art without love. Art is always the making of the soul, the craft of man's touch, whether that touch is corporeal or the touch of the mind and spirit—so it has been since Neanderthal times, and so it will always be.

November 4

The great value of knowing how to surrender is that any and all feelings can be let go of at any time and any place in an instant, and it can be done continuously and effortlessly.

What is the surrendered state? It means to be free of negative feelings in a given area so that creativity and spontaneity can manifest without opposition or the interference of inner conflicts. To be free of inner conflict and expectations is to give others in our life the greatest freedom. It allows us to experience the basic nature of the universe, which, it will be discovered, is to manifest the greatest good possible in a situation. This may sound philosophical, but, when done, it is experientially true.

November 5

The teeth of spiritual work occur when we are confronted with that which we cannot avoid. It is the direct confrontation that requires a leap in consciousness.

November 6

Although inherent to consciousness itself, context is usually not stated, identified, or defined. Therefore, there has previously been no actual science of truth itself, much less a means of verification or confirmation. So it is inevitable that humanity flounders and repetitively falls into endless disasters (such as repeating the same mistake over and over, hoping for a different result).

November 7

One mechanism the ego uses to protect itself is to disown any painful data and project it onto the world and others.

November 8

All reactions to life are subjective. There is nothing happening that is awful, exciting, sad, good, or bad. It is pointless to hold a position that catastrophes shouldn't "happen" or that the innocent didn't deserve it, or isn't it awful, or it must be somebody's fault. With a broad view, one can remain unperturbed by either the content or the context of life. That requires giving up judgments, expectations, or sensitivities.

November 9

It could be said that truth and reality represent an equivalence, and the validity of that equivalence can now be verified by reference to a calibrated scale of levels of truth that are objective, impersonal, and independent of the opinion of the observer. It is important to realize that *a statement of an alleged truth requires specification of context.*

November 10

True love is free of fear and characterized by non-attachment.

November 11

All life ebbs and flows. Everyone is born, suffers afflictions, and dies. There is happiness and sadness, catastrophe and success, increase and decrease. The stock market rises and falls. Diseases and accidents come and go. The karmic dance of life unfolds in the karmic theater of the universe.

November 12

An individual's level of consciousness is determined by the principles to which he or she is committed. To maintain progress in consciousness, there can be no wavering from principle, or the individual will fall back to a lower level.

November 13

A self-honest person is not prone to having his or her feelings hurt or "having a bone to pick" with others. Honest insight has an immediate benefit in the reduction of actual as well as potential emotional pain. A person is vulnerable to emotional pain in exact relationship to the degree of self-awareness and self-acceptance.

November 14

Spiritual commitment is energized by the alignment of the spiritual will with the attributes of Divinity, which are truth, love, compassion, wisdom, and nonpartiality. Devotion prioritizes one's life and attracts that which is of assistance. To be a servant of God is a dedication whereby the goal takes precedence over all other positionalities, attractions, or distractions.

November 15

Thoughts are like goldfish in a bowl; the real Self is like the water. The real Self is the space between the thoughts, or more exactly, the field of silent awareness underneath all thoughts.

November 16

Every forgiveness is a benefit to everyone. The universe notes and records every action and returns it in kind. Karma is actually the very nature of the universe because of the innate structure and function of the universe itself. In the universe, time is measured in eons. Beyond that, it doesn't even exist at all. Every kindness is therefore forever.

November 17

Spiritual work involves withdrawing attachment to, or identification with, content—and then progressively realizing that one's reality is context. The briefest explanation is that the self is content and the Self is context.

November 18

The critical point in all spiritual work is the capacity to be willing to tell the truth. Very often that truth is "I don't know," and out of the "I don't know" comes the willingness to surrender to God. The truth comes about through the act of surrender.

November 19

Excessive desire creates the illusion of lack, just like seeming money problems are created by spending faster than income.

November 20

Q: What does "surrender to God" really mean?

A: It means to surrender control and the secret satisfactions of the ego's positionalities. Turn only to love and to God as the source of life and joy. This choice is available in every instant. When finally chosen, the reward is great. By invitation, spiritual awareness illuminates the way. The key is willingness.

November 21

There is no opposite to the Allness, Love, and Totality of God. Unless one is unreservedly willing to surrender one's very life and die for God, then spiritual purification should be the goal of one's endeavor instead of enlightenment.

November 22

The ego relies on force; the spirit influences by power. Awareness knows that it is not what you do but who you are and what you have become that counts in the long run.

November 23

When that inner emptiness, due to lack of self-worth, is replaced by true self-love, self-respect and esteem, we no longer have to seek it in the world, for that source of happiness is within ourselves.

November 24

The world is actually entertainment. Like amusement, it is meant to be worn lightly. Heaven is within and is revealed by awareness. The world is merely an appearance. Its melodrama is an artifice of the distorted sense of perception. It leads one to think that the world is large, powerful, and permanent and that the Self is small, weak, and transitory; exactly the opposite is true.

November 25

The key to painless growth is humility, which amounts to merely dropping pridefulness and pretense, and accepting fallibility as a normal human characteristic of self and others.

November 26

Q: What about Judgment Day?

A: Man extrapolates the ego's qualities to God and then fears God. Judgment Day is every day; it is already here and is constant and unending.

November 27

Judgmentalism is the great vanity of all egos. Scripture says, "Judge not, lest ye be judged." Also, "Judgment is mine, sayeth the Lord." Christ said to forgive. The Buddha said that there is nothing to judge because perception can only see illusion. Perception is always partial and limited by an arbitrary context. In truth, no judgment is possible.

November 28

Value, from the ego's viewpoint, is an emotionalized mentalization, and Reality does not require mentalization. With humility, one can honestly state and witness that everything merely "is as it is," independent of projected worth. Its intrinsic "value" is that it "is"; that is, existence is complete within itself and is not needful of projected nominalization as "special." When the Divine Essence of All of Creation shines forth without obstruction, then the ego/mind goes silent in awe.

November 29

While it is obvious that there are many elements and forces in the world that are deleterious to human life and happiness, it isn't necessary to hate or demonize them—instead, merely make appropriate allowances and avoid them.

November 30

Once one becomes willing to give love, the discovery quickly follows that one is surrounded by love and merely didn't know how to access it. Love is actually present everywhere, and its presence only needs to be realized.

December 1

One of the laws of consciousness is: We are only subject to a negative thought or belief if we consciously say that it applies to us. We are free to choose not to buy into a negative belief system . . . By refusing to accept the negative belief, it now has no hold over our own life.

December 2

We influence others by what we are rather than by what we say or have.

December 3

Love is misunderstood to be an emotion; actually, it is a state of awareness, a way of being in the world, a way of seeing oneself and others. Love for God or nature or even one's pets opens the door to spiritual inspiration. The desire to make others happy overrides selfishness. The more we give love, the greater our capacity to do so. It is a good beginning practice to merely mentally wish others well throughout the course of the day. Love blossoms into lovingness, which becomes progressively more intense, nonselective, and joyful.

December 4

The destiny of the spirit will be, for better or worse, depending on the choices and decisions one makes.

December 5

Lovingness is a way of relating to the world. It is a generosity of attitude that expresses itself in seemingly small but powerful ways. It is a wish to bring happiness to others, to brighten their day and lighten their load. To merely be friendly and complimentary to everyone one meets in the course of a day is revealing.

December 6

The continuing grief over a loss is due to the resistance to accepting that state and allowing the grief to expend itself. The persistence of a feeling is due to the resistance to allowing it to be relinquished . . . Once we accept the fact that we can handle grief, we are already up into pride. The feeling of "I can do it" and "I can handle it" brings us to courage. With the courage to face our inner feelings and let them go, we thus move on to the levels of acceptance and eventually peace.

December 7

Experientially, guilt is an operational "reality" until the underpinnings of the ego are removed. Spiritual seekers are sometimes prone to look back critically on their past actions from their newfound spiritual position. All self-examination should be done with compassion, keeping in mind that past errors arose within a different context. The best resolution of guilt is to rededicate oneself to God and one's fellow man, and to the forgiveness of self and others.

December 8

Humanity is an "affliction" we're all burdened with. We don't remember asking to be born, and we subsequently inherited a mind so limited it is hardly capable of distinguishing what enhances life from what leads to death. The whole struggle of life is in transcending this myopia.

December 9

Attachments are illusions. They can be surrendered out of one's love for God, which inspires the willingness to let go of that which is comfortably familiar.

December 10

The spiritual information necessary for advanced states should be learned early and stored away for when it is needed. The possible downside of hearing advanced information early is the intellect's presumption of the prideful *I know that*. It is better to hold the information as *I have heard that*. To truly "know" is to "be," at which point one does not know; instead, one is.

December 11

The capacity for forgiveness arises from accepting with honest humility the limitations inherent in the human condition itself—which is, after all, merely on a learning curve of the evolution of consciousness.

December 12

There is no indication from any source of higher truth that God is influenced or assuaged by guilt. The great sages of history do not speak of guilt but instead refer to "sin" as being due to ignorance.

December 13

Attachment is a very peculiar quality of the ego. It can be totally undone in all its pervasive and multitudinous forms of clinging by simply letting go of one's faith in it or belief in its value as a reality. The attachment to "self" or "me" or "I" is a basic trap. One can seek out its fantasy value—the self gets attached to what it values.

Note that attachment requires and is sustained by an energy and an intention. The mind is attached to the very process of attachment itself as a survival tool. Letting go of the ego is based on the willingness to surrender attachment to it as a substitute for God.

December 14

The heart is the home of all courage. To be stout-hearted is to have the heart of the lion.

December 15

Nothing in the universe happens by chance or accident. The universe is a coherent concurrence and interaction of innumerable conditions attendant on the infinite number of energy patterns. In the state of awareness, all this is obvious and can be clearly seen and known. Outside that level of awareness, it could be likened to innumerable, invisible magnetic fields that automatically coalesce or repel one's position, and interact according to the positions and relative strengths and polarities. Everything influences everything else and is in perfect balance.

December 16

To understand the nature of God, it is necessary only to know the nature of love itself. To truly know love is to know and understand God, and to know God is to understand love.

December 17

Consciousness research confirms that death is not a possibility. Life itself is supported by its eternal source, from which it cannot be separated. That which is linear, circumscribed, and limited in time comes into existence because of what is eternal and nonlinear.

December 18

True strength is always accompanied by kindness, gentleness, and softness of expression. That position is one of choice and not one of compulsion.

December 19

The source of joy is always present, always available, and not dependent on circumstances. There are only two obstacles:

(1) the ignorance that it is always available and present; and

(2) valuing something other than peace and joy above that peace and joy because of the secret pleasure of the payoff.

December 20

The option for truth, peace, and joy is always available, although seemingly buried behind an ignorance and nonawareness that results from having chosen other options as a habit of thought. The inner truth reveals itself when all other options are refused by surrender to God.

December 21

Q: How should one best relate to the world?

A: To be "in" it but not "of" it. Remember that the world is a means and not an end. Nonattached interaction reveals habitual styles and attitudes that are consequent to inner ego positionalities.

December 22

To choose the love *for* God activates the love *of* God by prayer and worship.

December 23

The antidote to pride is to choose humility and integrity instead of a positionality such as being important or right, getting even, indulging in blame, or seeking admiration. All credit for accomplishment is given to God as the presence of the Divinity within instead of to the ego; therefore, accomplishment results in gratitude and joy rather than vulnerable pridefulness.

December 24

Human life subserves the spirit. The world is less painful to witness if it is appreciated as the ultimate school wherein we earn salvation and serve each other through our own lives.

December 25

The living proof of God's love and will for you is the gift of your own existence.

December 26

Thoughts in and of themselves are painless, but not the feelings that underlie them! . . . It is the accumulated pressure of feelings that causes thoughts. One feeling, for instance, can create literally thousands of thoughts over a period of time. Think, for instance, of one painful memory from early life, one terrible regret that has been hidden. Look at all the years and years of thoughts associated with that single event. If we could surrender the underlying painful feeling, all of those thoughts would disappear instantly and we would forget the event.

December 27

Realize that if you *are* something, there is nothing to understand about it. Reality is the ultimate in simplicity.

December 28

One basic principle has the power to resolve the problems of the social marketplace: support the solution instead of attacking the supposed causes.

December 29

When one willingly lets a hated perpetrator "off the hook" by forgiveness, it is not that person who is taken off the hook, but oneself.

December 30

Compassion arises from the acceptance of human limitation and by seeing that everyone is really the captive of his or her own worldview. With nonattachment, there is no longer the pressure to try to change the world or other people's viewpoints, or to make them wrong by virtue of disagreement.

December 31

Q: What is a workable goal?

A: To verify spiritual truth experientially and to *become it* rather than just conform to it. The process is an unfolding of discovery resulting in greater happiness and diminution of fear, guilt, and other negative emotions. The motive is inner development, evolution, and fulfillment of potential, which is independent of the external world. Life becomes progressive rather than just repetitive. All experience is of equal value and innately pleasurable so that life stops being an endless sequence of alternating pleasure and displeasure. With inner progress, context expands, resulting in greater awareness of significance and meaning—and, therefore, gratification of potential.

Glossary

This glossary is a composite of edited excerpts from Dr. Hawkins's work:

Consciousness: Consciousness is the irreducible substrate of the human capacity to know or experience, to perceive or witness, and it is the essence of the capacity for awareness itself. It is the formless, invisible field of energy of infinite dimension and potentiality, and the foundation of all existence. It is independent of time, space, or location, yet all-inclusive and all-present.

Consciousness is the unlimited, omnipresent, universal energy field, carrier wave, and reservoir of all information available in the universe—and, more important, it is the very essence and substrate of the capacity to know or experience. Even more critically, consciousness is the irreducible, primary quality of all existence.

Consciousness is an impersonal quality of Divinity expressed as awareness and is nondualistic and nonlinear.

It is like infinite space that is capable of awareness and a quality of the Divine essence.

Context: The total field of observation predicated by a point of view. Context includes any significant facts that qualify the meaning of a statement or event. Data is meaningless unless its context is defined. To "take out of context" is to distort the significance of a statement by failing to identify contributory accessory conditions that would qualify the inference of meaning.

Duality: The world of form characterized by seeming separation of objects, reflected in conceptual dichotomies such as "this/that," "here/there," "then/now," or "yours/mine." This perception of limitation is produced by the senses because of the restriction implicit in a fixed point of view.

Ego (or self with a small *s*): The ego is the imaginary doer behind thought and action. Its presence is firmly believed to be necessary and essential for survival. The reason is that the ego's primary quality is perception, and as such it is limited by the paradigm of supposed causality. The ego could be called the central processing and planning center—the integrative, executive, strategic, and tactical focus that orchestrates, copes, sorts, stores, and retrieves. It can be thought of as a set of entrenched habits of thought that are the result of entrainment by invisible energy fields that dominate human consciousness. They become reinforced by repetition and by the consensus of society. Further rein-forcement comes from language itself.

To think in language is a form of self-programming. The use of the prefix "I" as the subject, and therefore the implied cause of all actions, is the most serious error and automatically creates a duality of subject and object. Put another way, the ego is a set of programs in which reason operates through complex, multilayered series of algo-rithms wherein thought follows certain decision trees that are variously weighted by past experience, indoctrination, and social forces; it is therefore not a self-created condition. The instinctual drive is attached to the programs, thereby causing physiological processes to come into play.

Enlightenment: A state of unusual awareness that replaces ordinary consciousness. The self is replaced by the Self. The condition is beyond time or space, is silent, and presents itself as a revelation. The condition follows disso-lution of the ego.

Karma: In essence, individual karma is an information package (analogous to a computer chip) that exists within the nonphysical domain of consciousness. It contains the code of stored information that is intrinsic to, and a portion of, the spiritual body or soul. The core represents a condensa-tion of all past experiences, together with associated nuances of thought and feeling. The spirit body retains freedom of choice, but the range of choices has already been patterned.

Karma is linear, propagates via the soul, and is inherited as the consequence of significant acts of the will. Karma really means accountability—and, as cited in previous spiritual research, every entity is answerable to the universe. To summarize, as is commonly known, karma (spiritual fate) is the consequence of decisions of the will and determines spiritual destiny after physical death (the celestial levels, hell, purgatory, or the so-called inner astral planes [bardos]). Included also is the option of reincarnation in the human physical domain, which, by consciousness-calibration research, can only be done by agreement with the individual will. So all humans have, by agreement, chosen this pathway. In addition, consciousness research confirms that all persons are born under the most optimal conditions for spiritual evolution, no matter what the appearance seems to be.

Linear: Following a logical progression in the manner of Newtonian physics and, therefore, solvable by traditional mathematics through the use of differential equations.

Nonduality: When the limitation of a fixed locus of perception is transcended, there is no longer an illusion of separation nor of space and time as we know them. On the level of nonduality there is observing but no observer, as subject and object are one. You-and-I becomes the One Self experiencing all as Divine. In nonduality, consciousness experiences itself as both manifest and unmanifest, yet there is no experiencer. In this reality, the only thing that has a beginning and an ending is the act of perception itself.

Positionality: The positionalities are structures that set the entire thinking mechanism in motion and activate its content. Positionalities are programs, not the real Self. The world holds an endless array of positions that are arbitrary presumptions and totally erroneous. Primordial positionalities are: (1) *Ideas have significance and importance;* (2) *There is a dividing line between opposites;* (3) *There is a value of authorship—thoughts are valuable because they are "mine";* (4) *Thinking is necessary for control, and survival depends on control.* All positionalities are voluntary.

Self (capital S): The Self is beyond, yet innate in, all form—timeless, without beginning or end, changeless, permanent, and immortal. Out of it arises awareness, consciousness, and an infinite condition of "at home-ness." It is the ultimate subjectivity from which everyone's sense of "I" arises. The Infinite Reality does not even know itself as "I" but as the very substrate of the capacity for such a statement. It is invisible and all present. The Self is the Reality of reality, the Oneness and Allness of Identity. It is the ultimate "I-ness" of consciousness itself as the manifestation of the unmanifest. Thus, only can the indescribable be described.

Subjectivity: Life is lived solely on the level of experience and none other. All experience is subjective and nonlinear; therefore, even the linear, perceptual, sequential delineation of "reality" cannot be experienced except subjectively. All "truth" is a subjective conclusion. All life in its essence is nonlinear, nonmeasurable, nondefinable. It is purely subjective.

Truth: Truth is relative and only "true" in a given context. All truth is only so within a certain level of consciousness. For instance, to forgive is commendable, but at a later stage, one sees there is actually nothing to forgive. There is no "other" to be forgiven. Everyone's ego is equally unreal, including one's own. Perception is not reality. Truth arises out of subjectivity and is obvious and self-revealing. Truth is radical subjectivity. With the collapse of the illusions of duality, including the supposed "reality" of a separate "self," there remains only the state of the Infinite "I," which is the manifestation of the Unmanifest as the Self. Truth has no opposites, such as falsity or "off-ness." Nothing is hidden from the field of consciousness. The ultimate truth is beyond is-ness, beingness, or any intransitive verb. Any attempt at Self-definition, such as "I Am That I Am"—or even just "I Am"—is redundant. The ultimate reality is beyond all names. "I" signifies the radical subjectivity of the state of Realization. It is in itself the complete statement of Reality.

About the Author

Dr David R. Hawkins was director of the Institute for Spiritual Research, Inc., and remains a widely known authority within the field of consciousness research even after his death in 2012. He wrote and taught from the unique perspective of an experienced clinician, scientist and teacher, having been a life member of the American Psychiatric Association, with 50 years of clinical experience. His background and research are outlined in *Who's Who in America* and *Who's Who in the World*. He was honoured worldwide with many titles and he had been knighted and honoured in the East with the title 'Tae Ryoung Sun Kak Tosa' (Foremost Teacher of the Way to Enlightenment). Dr Hawkins lectured widely at universities (Harvard, Oxford, et al.) and to spiritual groups from Westminster Abbey and Notre Dame, and to Catholic, Protestant and Buddhist monasteries. His life was devoted to the upliftment of mankind.

www.veritaspub.com

Hay House Titles of Related Interest

YOU CAN HEAL YOUR LIFE, the movie,
starring Louise Hay & Friends
(available as an online streaming video)
www.hayhouse.com/louise-movie

THE SHIFT, the movie,
starring Dr. Wayne W. Dyer
(available as an online streaming video)
www.hayhouse.com/the-shift-movie

***

BECOMING SUPERNATURAL: How Common People Are Doing the Uncommon, by Dr. Joe Dispenza

BLISS BRAIN: The Neuroscience of Remodeling Your Brain for Resilience, Creativity, and Joy, by Dawson Church

POWER OF AWAKENING: Mindfulness Practices and Spiritual Tools to Transform Your Life, by Dr. Wayne W. Dyer

TRUST LIFE: Love Yourself Every Day with Wisdom from Louise Hay

All of the above are available at www.hayhouse.co.uk

***

CONNECT WITH
HAY HOUSE
ONLINE

🌐 hayhouse.co.uk   **f** @hayhouse

📷 @hayhouseuk   🐦 @hayhouseuk

▶ @hayhouseuk   ♪ @hayhouseuk

Find out all about our latest books & card decks • Be the first
to know about exclusive discounts • Interact with our authors
in live broadcasts • Celebrate the cycle of the seasons with us
• Watch free videos from your favourite authors •
Connect with like-minded souls

'The gateways to wisdom and knowledge
are always open.'

Louise Hay